Bullying Built Me!

Survival Guide for Women in the Workplace

*IvoryGrey Career Chronicles
Series One*

Ivy K. Ingram, Ed.S, CHLC, CCC

Copyright 2021 By Ivy K. Ingram

All Rights Reserved

Image and Elements: Canva Designs

Cover Design: Ivy K. Ingram

Layout: Ivy K. Ingram

Headshot Photo: StudyHall@7 A.M.

Printed in the U.S.A.

www.ivorygreycareer.com

Copyright All rights reserved. No part of this publication may be reproduced, distributed, or transmitted in any form by any means, including photocopying, recording, or other electronic methods without the prior written permission of the author, except in the case of brief quotations embodied in reviews and certain other noncommercial uses permitted by copyright law.

About the Author

Ivy Ingram is a certified life and career coach who strives to work with individuals to enhance their quality of life. With an educational background in Women's Studies, she is an advocate for women's rights. Ivy has a courageous spirit that drives her to speak out and bring awareness to "hidden" issues among women.

As an advocate of education, Ivy has earned her Bachelor of Arts Degree in Women's Studies, Master of Arts in School Counseling, and an Educational Specialist

Degree in Educational Leadership. In addition, she has earned a host of certifications and continues to seek professional development opportunities.

As a victim of bullying in several work environments in the past 15 years, Ivy decided to share some of her stories along with some strategies to help others. She felt obligated to give her experiences a voice and liberate others who have similar experiences. Workplace bullying is not a common conversation. It makes some people uncomfortable and others simply fearful. Then there are individuals like Ivy, who think to themselves, "Is it me? What am I doing wrong? It must be me." Upon discovering herself and coming into her own, Ivy realized that her years of suffering were not a result of her work performance or results. She realized that it was about who she was as a person. Her greatness, intelligence, work ethic, and overachieving personality intimidate others. Ivy also learned that she was not alone and what she had endured was not new under the sun. Her own mother was bullied for years in the workplace. As a coach and advocate, Ivy needed to empower others. She needed to free other victims. Most importantly, she needed to start the much-needed conversation and awareness of bullying in the workplace.

By way of New Jersey, Ivy is a native of North Myrtle Beach, South Carolina. She is a fan of music, loves to shop, and enjoys the beach. As a member of Delta Sigma Theta Sorority, Inc, Ivy values community service and sisterhood. She is a mother of one, Kyler, and a friend to many. Meet your author, Ivy K. Ingram.

Topics of Discussion

Acknowledgments

What is Workplace Bullying?

Different Shapes and Sizes: Bully Types

Document, Document

Kill Them with Kindness

Knowledge is Power! Know Your Rights

Identify A Battle Buddy

Speak UP, Speak OUT!

Some Hidden Truths About Your Bully

The Implications of Bullying

How my story ends…better yet, how my life began!

- Bonus Chapter: Bullying in the Midst of a Pandemic (March 2022)

Acknowledgments

I would like to first acknowledge my leader, healer, protector...my father, The heavenly Lord above. For He provided angels to accompany me as I navigated through the obstacles and barriers in the workplace. Allowing me to endure unpleasant experiences helped me to arrive at one of my many purposes. This book came to be as a result of what I thought was pure hell. I am forever grateful.

My mom, Christiana Ingram. For she carried, nurtured, mentored, and supported me. She accepted the assignment to not only birth me into this world but to raise me into the remarkable woman that I am today. A woman of integrity, hard work, determination, excellence, and pride...my mom has been a dynamic role model. Not once did I hear her complain as she experienced workplace bullying many years ago. I often thought about her as I sat in my car crying after work. If she could do it, so could I. I was cut from her tough cloth. Love my momma.

To my deceased grandparents. Lue Ethel and Roosevelt Murray. For the sacrifices, they made to assist my mother with providing for us. I learned many lessons from them as well. My grandfather modeled how to conduct myself in a mature, professional manner. My grandmother said, "You always do your best. Even if you clean toilets for a living, you be the best toilet cleaner you can be!" Love and miss you both.

To my Carolina Family. Only God knows how much I truly love you all. James and Fannie Carolina always saw something special in me. They felt the need to always protect me...like I was a diamond in the rough. At the tender of 7 when I met them, they embraced my quiet, sensitive spirit. Not allowing even my own momma to bother or upset me. They were the first to make me feel unique and special. It took many, many years to become self-confident and see what they saw in me. That I am truly unique and special. Love you both. Missing Father every day. Thanks for visiting Kyler and me on a weekly basis. Felicia Carolina Clemons. Yes ma'am! My #1 fan. She was my first fan as she always showered me with love and admiration. Always complimented me and made me feel pretty. She always compared me to Chilli from TLC. She also became my son's Nana. At one of my weakest moments in my short life, she showed up without hesitation and rocked my baby while I went to work every day. Leaving her own family behind, she moved in with me for the first year of his life ensuring that he was safe and loved. A love like no other. Words could never express how much I appreciate you. To her husband, Simon Clemons, thank for you embracing my son and giving him to opportunity to call someone Papa. Your support and push to be greater over the years has been invaluable.

Detria Carolina for always keeping me on my toes. Challenging my intellect with provoking questions and topics of discussion. We debate. Fuss a little. Then find some good music and snacks to share. It is a weird relationship. Love her bad. Jamie Carolina Turner for giving me my first taste of independence. Yes! Always confident and sure of herself. And when she got her license and a car, she took me on many adventures with her. Truly the big sister I never had. Exposing me to all kinds of things. Exposing me to life which helped to make me well-rounded. Oh, the good times. Tawanna Carolina for standing up for me on the school bus. I was about to fight somebody for being sassy to my mom, who was our bus driver at the time. Tawanna stood up and told me to sit down. "You got too much to lose. I got this!" Oh yes! You better be my big sister in a time of need. Sacrifice. I will never forget her willingness to sacrifice for me. NOW, I see what she saw as she said that I had too much to lose. Thank you, Wanna! And Rebecca Carolina AKA Red. My sidekick since we were seven years old. My quiet storm. Do not bother her and she will not bother you. As we grew up, we ended up with different sets of friends and unique college journeys. None of our differences ever mattered. I grew up to be loud and crazy. She remained mild and laid back. I will always appreciate how she loves me. She is the only person in my circle that lights up when she sees me. It is a special kind of love that we share. We can go weeks, months without speaking. Put us in the same room, it's like we never missed a beat. Rebecca keeps me grounded.

Tanya Redic and Tonya Jones...my TNT. Always had my back from the day we crossed the burning sands together. My line sisters are better than yours! TNT experienced similar walks in the workplace. So, it was important for me to lean on them throughout this journey. My fight was their fight. When I stood for me, I was standing for them as well. I love you both dearly. You all inspire me!

Kenyatta and Linda Jackson...my die-hard crew! Words cannot begin to express your role in my life. Thank you for loving on my son and me. Giving your all to us. You all cared for my baby when I had to go to work in the middle of a hurricane storm. I had to go to work or else I was risking my job. That chick probably would have written me up...again for not coming to work that day. Everyone else is safely at home with their loved ones while I am out weathering the storm trying to make it to the office. I cried, Lord I cried as I crossed the Jackson's front yard with my baby in my arms as the hard wind and rain beat me in the back. Wow! There's simply not enough I can say to express my gratitude for all these two women have done for me. From a temporary place to live to snacks in my cabinet to sheets on my bed...there is no way I deserved your devoted compassion. That is it. I am done. I cannot with you two!

Marielle Timmons...a mother of two at the time of my pregnancy. Donated her time to help me with my son. She would just show up after work. Sweeping the floors, taking out the trash, rocking my baby while I took a nap. Dropping off Sunday dinner. She is a fundamental part of my dark days. One of the reasons why I pushed when I wanted to give up. She even continued her encouragement as I endured many trying days at work. She would just randomly check on me to ensure that I was well and striving for my next. She believed in me as she looked up to me. Not realizing that I looked up to her. Admire her strength and tenacity. Mari had a little lamb, my rock!

Crystal Brantley...my sister soldier! She will straight up fight anybody that offends or comes for me. But, very nurturing. She has fed my son and me many days out of her kitchen. Always looking out. "Warm up your car. It's cold out" she would text me early some winter mornings. She is also responsible for my survival. During my maternity leave, I was not eating...I was scary skinny. I was so concerned with caring for my newborn that I would forget to eat. Crystal, Marielle, and The Gordon's made sure I ate. Without any of them, I probably would have faded away. Funny, not funny. Love you Crystal, my neighbor, my friend.

The Gordon family...my version of the Cosby's. Embraced me like I was one of their own children. They would scoop Kyler up out of my arms when I was in need, call and wake me up for church, pray with me, and stay ready to fight for me. Never wavered their love and faith in me. Very loyal folks. Down for me no matter what.

Salandra Bowman held me down during my last bullying experience. She would coach me as a professional and cuss with me as a friend. We talked many mornings on the way to work as I struggled to maintain my character in the workplace. Salandra is also my sorority sister, but she became my sister/friend first in college many moons ago. Not sure what I would have done without her guidance, support, prayer, and words of wisdom.

Leroy D. Gibson. While I found my voice at 18 at the University of South Carolina, Leroy helped me to find my silence. As he survived his own bullying experience, he was able to support and push me through my last experience. He would always say two infamous statements, "Watch, this thing is going to turn around." And…"You know you're going to be ok, right?" That wasn't a question. It was a statement. It was a fact. Leroy was also an outstanding friend, counselor, and support beam as I pushed through depression. He would not let me slip away. While on maternity leave, he would simply send me motivational quotes and check on me every day. He would just push. Nagged me until I expressed my emotions. Sent me gospel songs and scriptures for nighttime meditation. Lastly, Leroy believed in me
and encouraged me to bring out my greatness. He and Kenyatta would also fuss about how I failed to see what they saw in me. They push me so hard. Moreover, Leroy

would encourage me to hold my peace. To sit back and relax. I learned not to fight every fight. It was not necessary. God was totally in control and the battles were His. Thanks, Gibson.

My final acknowledgements. Darla Andrews and Cheryl Shepherd. Two of the strongest women that I have ever met. When I relocated to attend graduate school in Georgia, my mom said, "Find an older friend because women your age don't know any more than you know. All of you will be out there in the dark. Just dumb together." LOL! My mom talked hard, but it was from a good place. It did not make sense until I met Darla in Augusta, GA in 2008 and Cheryl in Florence, SC in 2013. Both are older, Caucasian women. They played a fundamental role in (pause for tears) my bullying experiences. I met both Darla and Cheryl in the workplace. They served as surrogate moms. Darla has one daughter and Cheryl have daughter. So, there was plenty of room for me! Countless days they held me in my office as I cried. Cheryl has even met me on the sidewalk and embraced me as I fell apart. Both had fight tears in their eyes as I described my bad days. Two momma bears had to hold back the blows they wanted to deliver to a couple of people who deemed it necessary to pick on me. I must note that, unlike several people, these ladies did not push me through my experiences. They sustained me. They kept me sane. They did not feel the need to address my past or plan my future. They sat and remained in the moment. They walked beside me and sometimes carried me. Prayed for me. She wrote me checks when I was broke and brought me lunch when I was hungry. (pause). Yeah, there are parts of me that now exist because of the unconditional love of Darla and Cheryl. There are parts of me that did not die because they fought for me to live.

To all my bullies. It is because of you I had the experiences and the fire in my belly to construct this book. THANK YOU! I am better, stronger, and wiser. You PUSHED me into GREATNESS!

What is Workplace Bullying?

"Ivy! (bangs on the desk) I'm writing you up! I hired secret shoppers and their feedback was not good for your area over there. People are applying to the college and haven't heard anything from your office. You have to tighten up over there. I mean it. And, and, and you know what??? I'm writing you up for approving leave for three people including yourself all last week. That's too many people off at one time. You know what? You have too many people working for you anyway. I'm not stupid. I know what goes on over there in that building. You need to get on board and straighten your area up."

Most of you have heard of bullying among children in schools and have a fair idea of what it means. Believe it or not, bullying in the workplace is very similar. Different tactics, but the impact on individuals is the same. Workplace bullying has not been formally defined, as it is difficult to put your finger on it. It is like a moving target.

However, I like the way Wikipedia (2018) explains it. "Workplace bullying is a persistent pattern of mistreatment from others in the workplace that causes either physical or emotional harm. It can include such tactics as verbal, nonverbal, psychological, physical abuse and humiliation. This type of workplace aggression is particularly difficult because, unlike the typical school bully, workplace bullies often operate within the established rules and policies of their organization and their society.

In many cases, bullying in the workplace is reported as having been by someone who has authority over their victim. However, bullies can also be peers, and occasionally subordinates. Research has also investigated the impact of the larger organizational context on bullying as well as the group-level processes that impact the incidence and maintenance of bullying behavior.

Bullying can be covert or overt. It may be missed by superiors; it may be known by many throughout the organization. Negative effects are not limited to the targeted individuals and may lead to a decline in employee morale and a change in organizational culture."

Let me introduce bullying in the workplace…

Can you relate?

#no2wkplacebullies
#letmewkinpeace
*https://en.m.wikipedia.org/wiki/Workplace_bullying

Different Shapes and Sizes: Bullying Types

Adult bullying can come in an assortment of forms. There are about five distinctive types of adult bullies.

A narcissistic bully is described as a self-centered person whose egotism is frail and possesses the need to put others down. An impulsive bully is someone who acts on bullying based on stress or being upset at the moment. A physical bully uses physical injury and the threat of harm to abuse their victims, while a verbal bully uses demeaning and cynicism to debase their victims. Lastly, a secondary adult bully is portrayed as a person that did not start the initial bullying but participates in it afterward to avoid being bullied themselves.

Serial bullying: The source of all dysfunction can be traced to one individual, who picks on one employee after another and destroys them, then moves on. Probably the most common type of bullying.

Secondary bullying: The pressure of having to deal with a serial bully causes the general behavior to decline and sink to the lowest level.

Pair bullying: This takes place with two people, one active and verbal, the other often watching and listening.

Gang bullying or group bullying: A serial bully with colleagues. Gangs can occur anywhere but, flourish in corporate bullying climates. It is often called mobbing and usually involves scapegoating and victimization.

Vicarious bullying: Two parties are encouraged to fight. This is the typical "triangulation" where the aggression gets passed around.

Regulation bullying: Where a serial bully forces their target to comply with rules, regulations, procedures, or laws regardless of their appropriateness, applicability, or necessity.

Residual bullying: After the serial bully has left or been fired, the behavior continues. It can go on for years.

Legal bullying: The bringing of a vexatious legal action to control and punish a person.

Pressure bullying or unwitting bullying: Having to work to unrealistic time scales and/or inadequate resources.

Corporate bullying: Where an employer abuses an employee with impunity, knowing the law is weak and the job market is soft.

Organizational bullying: A combination of pressure bullying and corporate bullying. Occurs when an organization struggles to adapt to changing markets, reduced income, cuts in budgets, imposed expectations, and other extreme pressures.

Institutional bullying: Entrenched and is accepted as part of the culture.

Client bullying: An employee is bullied by those they serve, for instance, subway attendants or public servants.

#beinformed
#adultbullyingisreal

https://en.wikipedia.org/wiki/Workplace_bullying

Document, Document!

Bullying of any kind can be difficult to prove. Workplace bullying is most certainly a challenge. Especially when most individuals in the workplace are adults. Many will either laugh, minimize your claim, or ignore you altogether. Therefore, you must document. Capture evidence to help shift your assumption to the facts! In other words, I can show you better than I can tell you.

Keep a few things in mind as you document and collect evidence. One, avoid getting in those trenches with your abuser. Maintain your class and integrity. By the time you start documenting, you are very emotional about the experience. Do not allow yourself to become too emotional. It will only cloud your judgment and ability to document appropriately. Emotions could lead you down a path of revenge. You do not want revenge; you will become the bully. You simply want to document what is happening to you. Remain professional and unbiased. Two, notate dates, times, and additional coworkers involved. Your documentation creates a story. It should demonstrate a series of events.

Types of documentation:
Emails
Conversations
Evaluations
Informal Reprimands
Formal Disciplinary Actions

You have to arm yourself. And you know what? It feels pretty good and empowering knowing you have that file tucked away. Feels really good!

"I asked Ivy to turn in her list prior to today's date. I even forwarded her the email from the district office as soon as I got it two weeks ago. I do not understand why she fails to meet deadlines. I mean, I know she's young, just graduating from college and all. I'm trying to work with her, but I do not know." I sit in front of the principal cool as a fan listening to my immediate supervisor roll the bus over me. She was called in and questioned about why my portion of the assignment was not sent to the district office on time. Then they called me in. Knowing my supervisor well, I kind of had a feeling about what the meeting was about. So I brought in my notes from previous staff meetings and the email that she indeed forwarded to me from the district administration. It was my turn to speak. I took a deep breath as I pulled out my email with the date highlighted. "Sir. I received this email two days ago, not two weeks ago. Here's my list as I have started working on it. However, everyone else was given two weeks, I was only given two days. No, actually, one day. She sent this email at 2:30 p.m. a day ago. We leave the office at 3:20 p.m. Now, she did mention in a staff meeting a month ago noted here in my minutes that she would make the entire team aware of the deadline as soon as she was made aware. Again, I just received my notification."

My immediate supervisor was so angry as she tossed and turned in her seat. I may have been young, but I was clever enough to document and save my email.

Also, keep in mind what you say in email communication. Do not get caught up. Your written documents, especially emails may be presented and read one day. You do not want to be just as guilty or have your claim discredited based upon how you have chosen to conduct yourself. With that being said, be mindful of how you go back and forth in emails with your bully. Be very careful and strategic when you craft your sentences. I have done two things before responding to an email. 1. I give it some time. Give myself an opportunity to relax and release my immediate emotions. 2. I have someone that I trust to proofread my emails before I send them. It never fails, they always find something that I need to rephrase or take out. Ha! There have been times when I am raw and just as nasty in my response. It was very important to get an opinion first. So know yourself. Know when to back away. Know when to just tell someone to write for you! I have done that as well. Save yourself! Just remember, you need to document.

#document
#proveit
#donotgetcaughtup

Kill Them with Kindness

My mom's advice is always to, "kill them with kindness". Kill= Make their spirit quiver. Do the opposite of what they expect you to do. Confuse the enemy.

Them= Your haters. The Bully.
Kindness= Being kind, cordial, and polite in spite of how you really feel.

Let me be clear before I continue, this does not mean that you have to be fake. It is not pretending, but it may consist of a little acting at times. Nonetheless, I am not suggesting that you compromise yourself. Be genuine and authentic. In all, simply be professional. Whatever you do, please avoid being petty.

"Good morning! How are you?" I speak to a bully as we pass each other in the hallway. She is not my supervisor, but she does not realize that I know that she is indeed a

behind the scene influencer. One who will throw rocks and hide her hand. Host secret meetings on the phone and
in her office in efforts to plot against others, especially me. She never did care for me. She had been with the organization for ten plus years before I arrived. She did not understand my sassy demeanor and high energy. Looked me up and down every morning trying to figure out why I chose to dress so nicely for work. "How's the baby?" She asked. "He's fine. Thanks for asking!" I respond as I walk away thinking, *"You know you don't care anything about me and my son. Stop It!"* Then I say, "Have a good day!"

Do not allow anyone to steal your joy! But, be prepared for every attempt to do so. The more joy you display, the more attacks you will endure. Crazy, I know. But, that is how the enemy works. It will lay back with a smile as it watches you walk around angry or upset. It will take pride as it sits back and watches that sad look on your face. Notice I said, lay back and sit. Take notice! The enemy is not as busy bothering you when it is winning. When you allow it to win. Watch it remain busy and attack you from every angle as you wear that smile on your face walking around with pep in your step. It cannot stand it. Remember, the mission is to kill, steal and destroy.

Show up and be a team player. Have a willing attitude and go with the flow. Do not let your slip show.

"Ivy...I need you to take on some high schools for recruitment." My new supervisor says to me as I have been serving as the director of my department for almost three years. As my co-worker for several years, she has never cared for me. As my new supervisor due to her promotion, she is on me like white on rice. And she does not waste any time calling the shots and making changes. I'm thinking, "she can't be serious...that's for the young folks. I don't feel like running those streets, recruiting." In response I say, " Yes ma'am, will do. Which schools would you like for me to take on?"

Go with the flow. Do not roll your eyes in a meeting. I do not care if your eyes start burning. Hold them still and focused. Do not tap out in a meeting and get on your phone. Remain engaged. Take "notes". Pay attention.

Trust me, I get it. You will not agree or like every idea. Your insides may die from a slow death as you have to follow a plan that failed four years ago and simply does not make sense. At the end of the day, why should you really be that invested? Does any of it belong to you? No. So give it to them. Let the bully have their way.

Do what is asked of you. Does your skill set, talents and education fit the bully's job description that he or she has defined for you? Ummm...probably not. Like most bullies, the objective at hand is to minimize you. So they will strip you of your major duties and responsibilities. Begin to treat you like an intern having you file papers or create spreadsheets. Do it! Do it with pride and excellence. As long as they do not touch your coins, do it! Like my Grandma once told me, "I don't care if you clean toilets for a living. You be the best damn toilet cleaner there is!"

Go with it! Go. With. The. Flow.

The enemy will not understand any of this. Especially when you can maintain this after they have reprimanded you with some crazy verbal warning or write-up. They are really perplexed when you can smile after a write-up. So keep your head up and keep it pushing. This, too, shall pass. #bekind #gowiththeflow

Knowledge is Power! Know Your Rights

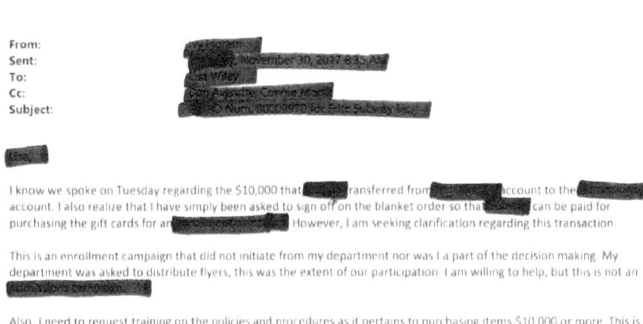

I know we spoke on Tuesday regarding the $10,000 that ▓▓ transferred from ▓▓ account to the ▓▓ account. I also realize that I have simply been asked to sign off on the blanket order so that ▓▓ can be paid for purchasing the gift cards for an ▓▓. However, I am seeking clarification regarding this transaction.

This is an enrollment campaign that did not initiate from my department nor was I a part of the decision making. My department was asked to distribute flyers, this was the extent of our participation. I am willing to help, but this is not an ▓▓.

Also, I need to request training on the policies and procedures as it pertains to purchasing items $10,000 or more. This is my first experience with spending and transferring this amount of money. As a budget manager who will be responsible for this money, I want to be certain that I am properly trained and competent before these funds are spent.

As an employee, government (state) or private, you have rights! If you were not aware of your rights before, now is the time to become aware. Several colleagues along with my supervisor were asking, no…demanding, that I sign off on spending $10,000 from the account that I managed. As noted in the email above, I knew it was out of order to spend that amount of money from my account. I most certainly was not about to sign off on it. After several hostile emails and phone calls, I refused to sign the paperwork. The money was spent anyway and the documents were moved forward without my signature. One thing I knew for sure, if I were called to the table to explain why I signed off such a large expense, I would be sitting alone. So I stood alone and said, No.

Email #2
From:
Sent:
To:
Subject:

I'm going to need you to sign this BO before they can start using it. I'll let them know and you get here as soon as you can. You must have forgotten this morning.

Email #5
From:
Sent:
To:
Subject:  DON'T FORGET WE NEED FOR YOU TO SIGN THE ▮▮▮▮ REQUISITION

Another moment in my career consisted of my supervisor targeting me. They simply did not feel that I was a team player. I was not what they wanted or needed me to be. I simply was not their cup of tea. So, they met with me on two occasions. One meeting was to conduct a verbal warning and the second meeting was to inform me that I had been officially written up. We met quite often to discuss my performance and lack of communication with my team.

So, a document, "the memo", is pushed across the table over to me for my review. I remember thinking, "all that I have done for this place and I'm looking down at a write-up?" This time last year I was honored as Staff Member of the Year! Now, I am being accused of inappropriate behavior and bad judgment? My mind was blown. Attempting to read the document, it took everything in me not to cry. Not to scream. Not to jump on the table. Kick over the table. Not to downright fight. I felt attacked as my leadership ability, work ethic, and character was being questioned. To be talked to like an unruly child. "I don't know what else to do. You need to get on board. I need my job. I am not sure if you need yours." Oh okay. My supervisor was so out of order and crossing the line. "Are you threatening to fire me?" I asked. Knowing my rights, my supervisor could not threaten me. I did not sign that document that insulted me and dismissed my accomplishments as an employee. It was a piece of paper that attempted to devalue me as a person and crush my career.

"Employee refuses to sign"

My supervisor noted this on the document. Why did I refuse to sign it? I was not made aware of my supervisor's expectations prior to the meeting. I had to be given a true opportunity to fail. Being reprimanded and informed of the rules at the same time is not fair. Quite frankly, it is ridiculous and poor leadership.

Know your rights. Be Powerful. Be Bold. Be Empowered.

#knowyourrights

#donotbepushedaround

#employeesmatter

Identify A Battle Buddy

"Hey...I need for you to meet me on the sidewalk with my purse and keys. I just exited stage left out of a nasty meeting. I need to go home." My friend/co-worker approaches me on the sidewalk as I wobble slowly towards her...I was about 7 months pregnant. I could not get to her fast enough. A bully who was my colleague had verbally attacked me, a pregnant woman, in a meeting. My supervisor at the time was so shocked and outdone, I do not believe that she knew what to do or say. So she just dismissed all of us from her office. Falling into my co-worker's arms, all I could do was cry in her bosom. All she could do was hold me as she repeatedly asked, "What did they do to you?" I could not stop crying long enough to share. I was emotional, pregnant, hungry, and exhausted. My feet and eyes were swollen. I just needed to remove myself from that toxic atmosphere.

There is a reason why the military highly recommends and often requires that enlisted soldiers have a battle buddy. Along this journey we call life, everyone needs at least one person of devoted support. No one should travel and navigate through life alone. So, I suggest that you do the same in the workplace. Find a battle buddy.

Working in an unhealthy work environment can often feel like you are at war. You will value having someone to run to when the going gets tough. You will need someone to listen when you need to vent. Get it out. Express your thoughts and feelings. Do not hold anything inside as it will only build up. And as you know, pressure will bust pipes. You need to be able to trust that this person will not share your conversation with anyone and not judge you as you may express some intense thoughts.

Your battle buddy must also be a good balance. You all cannot be crazy at the same time. Ha! There will be times when you are unraveling, at the point of losing it. You have just envisioned yourself turning over a table or slapping your bully. Opt to refrain from either of those violent acts. Instead, find or call your battle buddy. He or she will know that it is their time to remain calm and save you the humiliation of being escorted off the premises. They should help you to be rational and be able to provide an alternate solution to the problem at hand.

At the same time, out the other side of my neck, I am going to suggest that battle buddy be down for the cause as well. There will be times when you will have to talk him or her off the ledge. Yes, oh yes, they need to get highly upset about how you are being treated. Let me note that they may be enduring abuse from the same bully.

(Call a friend) "Come and pick me up. I need to get out of here." Standing outside my office building, pacing through the grass. "I'm not doing good." I just wanted to fulfill my first reaction to what happened to me...fight. As my friend drives me away from "bully lane", I'm silently staring out the window rubbing the anger energy out of my right leg. We rode in complete silence until my co-worker/friend turned on some Gospel music.

Finally, she says, "Think about your son." I begin to simmer down. Then she says, "This will not last because it's not right. You just have to weather the storm. All giants fall. It's going to be okay." Proceeds to turn the music up a little louder and we ride. #battlebuddy #callafriend

Speak UP, Speak OUT!

As others often complained to a good friend of mine, he would listen, and then ask, "So what are you going to do about it?"

Are you just going to sit there and take it? You may be concerned about retaliation if you speak up and report what is happening to you. Keep in mind, you have rights.

At this point, you have documentation to prove your claim. So, take what you have to your Human Resources department, present your information and ask for guidance. While you are there, inquire about free counseling services. I took advantage of our employee program that paid for four therapy sessions. I do not regret seeking that help at all. Speak up and acknowledge that you need to talk to someone...get on somebody's couch. The stress of a tainted workplace can be very taxing. So, whatever you do, avoid losing yourself throughout this journey.

Now that you have the tools and direction, follow through. Submit the report. Call the number. For God does not give us the spirit of fear. Pull back the covers and bring awareness. One thing I learned during my journey was the number of people who had suffered from bullying and intimidation by the same person as me. I also learned that other people were being bullied by other supervisors. So at this pivotal moment in your life, you will speak out for yourself and others. Be a leader! Be courageous! Use your voice!

Your Voice! Even if you decide to avoid filing any official letters or reports, speak out! Share with others what is going on and share your journey. If you cannot do anything else as an end result of your bullying experience, help someone else. Many people feel alone; they suffer in silence and try to survive on their own. It helps to know that you are not alone.

#speakupspeakout
#useyourvoice

Some Hidden Truths About Your Bully

As long as I kept thinking something was wrong with me, the experiences were very personal. I have been a victim of some form of bullying in the workplace four different times. FOUR! Each time I questioned myself. "What is so wrong with me that he/she feels the need to treat me this way?" All I ever wanted to do was to be excellent in all that I do. I am an overachiever, I am very structured, I prefer order, and I value professionalism. I inherited my work ethic from my family. I never intended to show anybody up by the way I dress for the workplace. It was not my mission to surpass goals in an effort to embarrass others who did not meet their goals. I certainly did not mean to step on anyone's toes as I spoke up in meetings to provide the correct information when incorrect data was provided. I was just being me! Ivy. That is all I know to do. Every morning when my feet hit the floor, I simply strive to be better than I was the day before. I am not in competition with anyone other than myself. Right?!? Surely you feel the same way and giving me an AMEN as you read my rant. I get it. I do. I understand you as you now understand me.

So let me take that load off your shoulders. Your bullying experience is not solely about you. Solely. I will deal with that in the next chapter. Listen to this. PAUSE. Clear your mind of all self-doubt as you have questioned yourself many days and hours on the job. Just breathe. Now imagine that your bully is sitting in front of you. And take a good look at him/her. Come on. Come with me. Close your eyes and see him/her. Now…let me enlighten you. They bully you because they were or are currently being bullied too. Breathe. They, too, were pushed around, minimized, and taunted by someone. Whether it was a parent, peer, spouse, or co-worker, they were taken advantage of, abused, and/or harassed. I am not asking you to feel sorry for him/her. And maybe you do. That is okay. But, more than anything I am asking you to embrace that reality. Ever heard that a child bully is being bullied at home? Yeah, more than likely they are. The same is true for adults.

Now, let me expose a few more possible truths about a bully. They are missing something that you possess. Something that they wish they had and resent you every day for it. In their mind, "I wish I could present like him." So, they say things like "I know how much you like to talk in front of people." With such sarcasm. Or they will deny your request to attend and present at a professional development conference. This is called insecurity. Most bullies are very insecure. And guess what? That is not your fault. There is something about you that attracts them to you. Something they desire to attain if only they could. Since there is only one you, they cannot have what belongs to you. So, they not only hate you for it, but they will strive to kill that very thing that they just cannot have. Do you want my joy? You cannot have it. Do you want my smile? You cannot have it. Do you want my style? It belongs to me. Do you want my gift? God gave this particular gift to me. They struggle to embrace their own gifts and talents. Instead, they focus on what they do not possess and identify it as their weakness. Why? At that point, in their mind, you have more than what they have. Therefore, you can outdo them. You are somehow better than them. Not realizing that you do not have it all either!

Another secret not far behind insecurity is self-esteem. As arrogant as many bullies will present themselves to be, they lack esteem. They question themselves all the time. Trust me! They have the same doubts that they have now planted in your mind. They are not as confident on the inside as they demonstrate on the outside. The insecurity about the attributes that your bully lacks leads to low self-esteem. I know it may not seem like it as you see your bully strut around the office with his/her chest out. That confidence comes from the mere fact that they have been empowered along the way. Someone believes in them. Therefore, they support their decisions and encourage their behavior. In addition, the bully has observed and identified that there are several employees that are intimidated by them. So as the roster of supporters and those who feel inferior increases, the bully feels empowered. They are getting away with bullying! Their tactics are working and they are getting their way. But, do not be distracted by that empowered strut. They are struggling underneath that empowerment.

They are powerless seeking power. They are cowards seeking bravery. They are weak seeking strength.

Bullies have issues just like everyone else. However, they often lack the coping mechanisms to deal with, heal and push through their issues. Many of them lack the ability to take accountability. So it is everyone's fault, but their own. No one can grow as long as they are blaming others for their mistakes, faults, or shortcomings.

Your bully has a past. Just like you do. But, oftentimes their past includes being bullied themselves. Either by a family member, school teacher, or family friend. There may also be some kind of abuse in their past. You may be thinking, "So do I!". Everyone is not wired the same. Each person is uniquely made. We do not handle trauma or unfortunate situations the same. Those who were bullied are especially likely to bully others. It is a learned behavior. Or it is a way to get you before you get me.

Lastly, bullies tend to be very paranoid. So you will experience what I like to call "get you, got you". It becomes an office theme or culture. It is a seed that is planted, water, and grows wild as everyone will begin to function this way. You may have received and viewed emails that copied everyone in the organization in an effort to put a colleague on the chopping block. Bullies eventually become fearful that someone will try to get them fired or "in trouble" just like they are doing on a daily basis. As the bully spends hours plotting against others, they begin to think about how they may be someone's target. So, you may hear and see accusatory behaviors. Often. Quite often.

Know this. You are not the only one the bully picks on. You probably are not the first and will not be last. As long as they have issues that are unresolved, they will continue to bully once you are long gone. As long as they are broken and hurt, they will continue to hurt others. Why? Because hurt people hurt people.

#hiddenissues
#itsnotalwayspersonal

The Implications of Bullying

Congratulations! You have walked away from the fire without smelling like smoke. Beauty does evolve from ashes. Meet the new you!

Even if you are currently enduring the experience, you will one day walk away (and soon) or the bully will be removed. Just hang in there.

Your bullying experience should have been good for you. Note. I did not say that it was good for you. It never feels good. Never. Actually, it sucks. How do you think it feels to the caterpillar that transformed into a butterfly? How did the bird feel when it hit the ground after the big push from the nest? OUCH! Growing hurts. Crazy? Yeah, I know. I thought so as well when it was revealed to me. In fact, I rejected it. Good for me? Huh? No one deserves such treatment. Trust. You are not placed in any situation by chance. Nothing in life is in vain. So take this time to self-reflect. Think about how this experience has impacted you. Sure, there may be some negative impacts. So pause here. Take a few minutes to deal with those negative effects. Bitter. Reluctant to trust. Lack self-esteem. The decline in morale. Decrease in focus. Lost motivation. Just to name a few, right? I completely understand. One of my experiences caused me to move everything out of my office! Totally depersonalize my space. Transferred all of my family pictures to a box and moved them to my living room at home. "I will never be loyal to another employer." As I walked to my car one evening with my box of personal belongings. I know the thoughts and feelings all too well.

Now, time for a mindset shift. Reach down and pull out all that you have learned from this experience. How did you evolve as a person? As a professional? What are your positive gains? Are you struggling a little? I did too at first. I will help you by sharing how I was tested and groomed. I learned to be quiet. I would sit in bizarre meetings and speak only when spoken to. It was very challenging, especially when my inner man was kicking and screaming, "this is so wrong!". It was not necessary to fight every battle. I had to let some situations play out as some things would work in my favor down the road. I immediately learned self-control and patience. Were they just handed over to me? "Here take these two pills tonight. You will be calm and patient in the morning." No. It does not work like that at all. I was consistently placed in situations that would test me. Day after day, meeting after meeting, I was tried. I was pushed. I was pulled. I was stretched!

Trust me. You will come out on the other side of this. You will be better for it. This sucks. It really sucks. It is stressful and challenges you. However, you are growing. I encourage you to grow better, not bitter. Bullying in the workplace will and can make you bitter. You will have the desire to build walls and keep others out. You may lose your joy and put your vibrant personality on a shelf. No! Do not lose who you are. You were made when you arrived to that workspace. It did not make you, therefore it can not break you.. Unless you let it. Instead, I say allow it to tear you down only to build you up. What feels like a setup is really a come up. So start focusing on yourself. Reflect. Grow. Prepare. Do not exist in the world of bullying. Thrive!

How my story ends...
better yet, how my life began!

My first bully encounters lead me to graduate school and relocate to another city. I had to jump. It was sink or swim. I turned in my two-week vacant notice to my landlord and my two-week notice to my employer. I applied to a school counseling program, submitted applications for a new job, and made a down payment on a new apartment. My cousin and my best friend from high school packed me up. And in a U-haul truck with all of my belongings, we head to a place of uncertainty. I was waiting to hear back from everyone. I had not been accepted to grad school, no one had called me for an interview and I did not have a place to live. Forty-five minutes down the road, we received a call with good news. Approval for the apartment. I had jumped and landed. Although I eventually found myself in my second bullying environment, I earned my master's degree, accomplished my longtime goal of becoming a member of Delta Sigma Theta, and I purchased my first home. All of these accomplishments resulted from being pushed by bullies in the workplace.

My third experience with a bully encouraged me to start my own small business. I turned my hobby of crafting into a business. I also decided to attend graduate school earning my third degree, an educational specialist in educational leadership. My crafting business, "The Touch by Ivy" did not live long, but it gave me a taste of entrepreneurship. It was the beginning of a mind shift.

Prior to my last bullying experience, I was already a certified life coach working with a few clients. I had planned and hosted a few women empowerment workshops. Then I was pressed to evolve and take my life to the next level. I eventually established two additional businesses, I became a first-time mom, I wrote this book and I am currently working on my doctorate degree.

In all, each experience was an opportunity to grow, evolve and enhance my life. Push. Pull. Push. Pull. Each season I was elevated. Just when I thought God had forgotten about me, He showed up. I am who I am today because of my bullying experiences. When I left my mother's home to attend college at the age of 17, I just knew I was ready to take on the world. I thought I had all the answers. I thought I was fully baked and that I had arrived. Although I was not sure of myself at the time, I had goals and plans as to how I would achieve them. Ha!

As I navigated the workforce, each bully pulled out the instruction manual and proceeded to break me down. I was humiliated, broken, abused, targeted, and harassed. In private places, I kicked, screamed, threw punches in the air, and cried. Many days, I cried. I would be pulled apart and moved down the assembly line to the next bully. At the end of the line, I was restored, rebuilt, and rejuvenated. I walked with pride in my walk, God in my smile, and peace in my heart. God had shown me who I was in Him and my purpose. He reassured me that I was just passing through. I had no clue that I was being stripped and pulled apart only to one day say…. Bullying Built Me.

Bonus Chapter:
Bullying in the Midst of a Pandemic

At the onset of a pandemic, which was initiated by the Coronavirus (COVID-19), many professionals found themselves working from home. While working from home always existed, the number of individuals including students, worked and learned from the comfort of their homes. In March of 2020, most of the nation closed businesses and schools in an effort to address the spread of the foreign virus. As all of us were packing up our office supplies to establish a workspace at home, many of the unfavorable aspects of the job went home with us. Bullying in the workplace was one of them. Seems odd, huh? Odd to me as well.

As a career coach, my clientele doubled from 2020 to 2021. Not only were professionals seeking new opportunities and purpose, but many of them also simply wanted advice on how to handle unwanted treatment from colleagues and supervisors. While many think that bullying cannot happen unless you are actually in the workplace, it happens in remote spaces more than we think.

"Yes, she can work from home, but we will need a list of her duties and responsibilities while she is out." I recall having to work from home once after we were called back into the workplace. My son's school was closed for a week due to a high number of positive COVID-19 cases. –Make a list of my duties and responsibilities? Really? As if my role changes because I am working within the confinements of my home. Now, let me be clear, this was not a form of bullying, nor did I feel pressured to fulfill some extreme task. However, I did feel a lack of trust and I certainly did not feel like the professional that I proclaimed to be my entire career.

This was only a taste of what others were enduring as they worked from home. I had a brief conversation with a professional who worked for a large corporation for three years. Now that she was working remotely, she found herself working more than she did when she reported to the physical building every day. She stated, "I feel like my supervisor piles more work on me now that I am home to ensure that I am *actually* working. She also fails to offer instructions or support and expects a short turnaround with daily progress updates. It's ridiculous!" This is an example of "The Scheming Bully", one who happens to be a manager. One who plots and devises a plan to abuse his or her power. While often dumping their work on their subordinates.

According to Indeed (2022), "If the bully is a manager, they may abuse this power by giving an employee undesirable shifts, excluding them from important meetings, or assigning them many difficult and time-consuming projects with little to no guidance on how to complete them."

The abuse of power and unfair treatment is bullying. Especially when it leads to emotional, psychological, and/or physical distress. The professional, "Sarah", was so overwhelmed, working 10-12 hours a day that she finally resigned. I asked, being the advocate that I am,

"Did you talk to your supervisor? Did you report it to Human Resources?" Sarah responded, "It would be my word against his. My coworkers see it, but they will not have my back. They need their jobs just as much as I do. But, I couldn't take it anymore. It was impacting my mental health."

Many individuals like Sarah experienced being overworked with unrealistic deadline expectations. In addition, professionals have reported being mistreated in virtual meetings and written up for not turning their cameras on (not knowing it was a new rule or expectation). Jobs have been threatened by call center professionals if they take a break or if their young child is heard in the background on calls. A number of violations take place in the homes of employees. As a matter of fact, bullying happens more frequently due to the fact that most of the interaction between the managers and team members or among colleagues happens one on one. This can be either via email communication or virtual meetings. The risk of having an audience or better yet, witnesses decreases in remote spaces. A Monster writing contributor denotes the following:

> Virtual misconduct is on the rise in remote work settings, says Joan Dunlop, a workplace investigations lead and partner at Cenera HR and Business Consulting in Calgary. When work and private life blend, work environments often get less formal, and professionalism can slip. Throw in COVID exhaustion, job instability, and stress, and you've got a breeding ground for bad behaviour. "Consequently, we see a rise in complaints of virtual harassment, discrimination, and bias amongst remote teams," she says.

Virtual misconduct! Wow. Not sure if you have heard that term before, but that is a new one for me. I am enjoying the conversations about bullying in the workplace and now, virtual misconduct. My hope is that the conversation will grow legs and take off running towards more policy manuals. I look forward to the day that anti-bullying policies and procedures are common. A day where workshops are coordinated to allow professionals to learn more about sensitivity and managers are trained on how to handle the matter if it is reported. The day when more employers are less tolerant of the behavior and encourage employees to report. I believe that we are getting there one day at a time. While bullying certainly helped to shape me as a professional, I am striving to prevent unforgettable experiences for others.

References

Indeed Editorial Team. *How To Manage Workplace Bullying (With Examples)*. (2022)
https://www.indeed.com/career-advice/career-development/workplace-bully?aceid=&gclid=Cj0KCQiAmpyRBhC-ARIsABs2EAqc5PiHLaHLmnaizyv-Dan2UMmz_iDj9pvtzbOc2MBc57by4cgeBigaAkxTEALw_wcB

Richard, Joanne. (n.d.). *Workplace bullying has gone remote: When work and private life blend, work environments often get less formal, and professionalism can slip.*
https://www.monster.ca/career-advice/article/workplace-bullying

Wikipedia.
https://en.m.wikipedia.org/wiki/Workplace_bullying

www.ingramcontent.com/pod-product-compliance
Lightning Source LLC
Chambersburg PA
CBHW021909170526
45157CB00005B/2033